Out of Idaho

Fiction, Poetry, & Nonfiction by

Grove Koger

Finishing Line Press
Georgetown, Kentucky

Out of Idaho

ACKNOWLEDGMENTS

"The Upstairs Room" originally appeared in the Cabin / Writers in the Attic
anthology *Rooms*.
"1953'" "Offerings;" "Jones Bros.;" "1968;" and "Where" originally appeared
in *Cold-Drill*.
"The Three Musketeers" originally appeared in *Gypsophila*.
"Wrecking Ball" originally appeared in *Red Ochre Lit* and was reprinted in
In-Flight Literary Magazine.
"A View of the Owyhees" originally appeared in *Cirque*.
"What I Mean?" originally appeared in *Man in the Street* and was reprinted
in *Subjectiv* [sic].
"The Other Side" originally appeared in *Flights*.

Publisher: Leah Huete de Maines
Editor: Christen Kincaid
Cover Art: Margaret Koger
Author Photo: Margaret Koger
Cover Design: Elizabeth Maines McCleavy

Order online: www.finishinglinepress.com
also available on amazon.com

Author inquiries and mail orders:
Finishing Line Press
PO Box 1626
Georgetown, Kentucky 40324
USA

Contents

Dedicated to the Memory of My Parents

The Upstairs Room

When I was young, I spent a summer up north.

It was a birthday gift, Mother explained, and as Aunt Bonnie and Uncle Arnold had no children of their own, they would be overjoyed to have me live with them for a time. Later I realized that the former statement was a subterfuge and the latter untrue. My parents were going through one of their rough patches, as Mother admitted toward the end of her short life, and whatever reasons lay behind my relatives' lack of offspring, the pair did not seem to take any particular pleasure in my company.

I headed north a week after I turned ten, entrusted to the care of a distracted bus driver. The swaying motion of the bus was worrying, and while the restaurant food I sampled in the middle of the day at our lunch stop was exciting (a club sandwich, of all things), it nevertheless settled in a lump in my stomach.

At the Coeur d'Alene bus station, a vaguely familiar, heavily perfumed woman hugged me and her balding companion shook my hand in a very formal way—and that, as far as I remember, was the last time that Arnold paid any attention to me. I sat in the back seat of their blue Buick while he drove away with great care and Bonnie, sitting beside him, talked on and on in a sharp voice. How were my mother and father? Did I like school? Did I have a girlfriend? (I didn't, and I was embarrassed to have to say so.)

Bonnie and Arnold's brick house was built on a low rise set back from the street. After easing the car into a garage in back, Arnold vanished and Bonnie led me in and up two flights of stairs.

"We don't use this floor often," she said as she opened a door, "but Maid has dusted your room thoroughly. I'm sure you miss your parents, but you're going to have a wonderful time here. Now if you'd like to rest"—here she glanced at a clock that ticked away on a chest of drawers—"we'll have dinner in an hour."

Then she set my suitcase down inside the door and I was alone. But not quite. Never before had a room welcomed me, but as I looked around me, a kind of tingling joy rose up my spine and down my arms to my fingertips.

The room was shaped like an L in reverse, and had a window at each end. One looked out through the limbs of a luxuriant tree and down the street, the other into the crowns of two other trees shading the garage. A twin bed sat near the corner of the L, and besides it and the chest of drawers, the room contained a straight back chair and a standing closet. I sat down on the bed, bathed in green light from the windows, and as I breathed in and out, the room seemed to breathe with me.

#

I had brought several books with me that summer, but for once, words on the page seemed less real to me than my surroundings. Maid (I'm ashamed to say that I never learned her name) or Bonnie walked down with me to the lakeshore some mornings after breakfast, and over time I'd put together quite a little collection of small snail and clam shells. Other mornings I just poked around in the big yard, climbing trees and peering in, as surreptitiously as I could, the neighbors' windows.

But early afternoons and evenings after dinner were reserved for the room. Muffled footfalls and murmured conversations reached me from below, but upstairs there were the never-ending songs of robins and blackbirds and—a little farther off—the raucous cries of gulls. The smells of summer flowers blew in gently on the breeze. As evening came on, insects in the trees joined the chorus. Small, white moths batted gently against the screens until I turned out the lights. And then there were the odd, unexpected sounds that I was never able to identify.

When I got home late that summer, after another long and disorienting bus ride, I was torn between wanting to explain and being afraid to, but under Mother's questioning I made an effort to tell her about Aunt and Uncle and the house and, especially, my room. I wasn't a bit lonely there, I finally blurted out, and tried to find words to describe how welcome the room had made me feel.

"My goodness," Mother said with a smile, "you make it sound like your room was haunted!" Then she went on to talk of other things. I could tell that she was still preoccupied, although I didn't learn why until much later.

As it turned out, I didn't see North Idaho again for another three decades, and, as time went by, I visited the upstairs room less and less often in my memory.

Mother died a few years after that summer, a war came and went, and Father remarried. I was moderately successful in business, a little less so in life. Then one afternoon a certified letter reached me from Coeur d'Alene. Arnold must have grown careless in his older age, for one evening he had driven Bonnie and himself off the road into the lake. And I must have made a better impression than I realized, because the house was now mine.

At this point you can probably anticipate the end of my story. The city had grown, but to my eye, it seemed less mysterious. When I pulled up in front of the house, I could have sworn that it had shrunk. The brickwork that had impressed me so much was stained and the trees around it had grown ragged and weedy. Staring up from the street, I realized that my room must once have been an attic.

The attorney waiting for me at the door suggested that I would want to take a careful look around the house before making any decisions. Perhaps I would, I thought, but I told him that I might not be long. Then with trepidation I made my way up the creaking stairs—to a door that stuck and a room that was low-ceilinged and dusty. There was no furniture, and the window screens were choked with years of dust and debris.

Aside from the room's forlorn appearance, I was overwhelmed by a negative quality as I stood in the doorway—the utter *absence* of something. Despite Mother's offhand comment so many years before, I had never thought that there had been some unnatural presence in the room. But now I realized quite clearly that there *had* been *something* here, once, and that it was no more. Whatever—no, *whoever*—had once dwelt here had long since departed.

I closed the door softly and headed back down the stairs to tell the attorney my decision.

1953

My father still plowed
with a team. It was
my job to ride the white mare
and scatter the gulls. Did
he dream of that black,
unfolding earth all those
years he lay dying? I know
one of us did.

The Three Musketeers

This is a true story.

Three children—John, Dale, and Beth—grew up near each other on farms south of town, and if you'd asked them later, in their teens, they would have said that they'd known each other forever. They played together and fooled around together without quite knowing what they were doing and ate lunch together at one house or another and went into town together for Saturday matinees at the town's only theater when one parent or another could give them a ride. Along with everybody else, their parents called them the Three Musketeers, and they reveled in the sound of it, the *feel* of it, although only John, who was starting to read a lot, actually understood the reference or realized, a little vaguely, that these Musketeers lacked their d'Artagnan.

Then, at some point that none of them could be sure of, or even gave much thought to, they started to grow up. Dale and Beth started dating seriously and then going steady a few months later, and since Dale saved up and got himself a blue 1964 Mustang GT and a temporary license about that same time, it was pretty easy for them to get away by themselves. But they remained friends with John, even though he and his parents had moved to a farm north of town, and every couple of months Dale and Beth would pick up John in Dale's Mustang and the three of them would head out to a bluff overlooking the river and the Boise Front to drink Coors or Budweiser and talk and listen to the crickets busy in the bushes around them and the occasional bobcat crying hoarsely as it made its way along the river far below.

John knew that those crickets were actually little pale green tree crickets, not the black ground crickets that everybody thought of when you said "crickets," and he might have said so sometime, but he didn't. There wasn't any point. He knew, of course, that what

Beth and Dale *really* wanted was to be alone, and his frustration and desire grew into a tighter knot every time he looked at them.

And that's how things stood the last night they got together, the very last night, out there on the bluff. They'd be seniors next year, and what with the summer ahead, their talk was a little unfocused. Time was passing and things were changing. Dale would be working full-time on his neighbors' farm that summer, and Beth would be putting in more hours at the drive-in out on Logan, and she was pretty sure that Dale would be proposing sometime, and that was about all she could think about. And John? Well, John knew he ought to get a job but he couldn't see how, since he didn't have a car and didn't know what anyone would want to hire him to do. Plus his parents were insisting that he apply to college, which set him even more apart in their little farming community, so he didn't talk much that night. It all felt like the end of something.

And then suddenly it was later than any of them had realized. Beth's parents were pretty open-minded, but they were also big on observing the proprieties and they expected Dale to get their only daughter home by a decent hour, so the three of them jumped up (startling those crickets into silence) and got ready to go. John's house was only about a mile away, so he volunteered to walk home—an offer that Dale and Beth accepted a little too readily.

So after helping Dale and Beth shake out the blanket they'd been sitting on and dump the empties in a ravine, John started out down the dirt road in the moonlight, planning to climb into his bedroom window when he finally got home, and Dale and Beth piled into the Mustang and took off, Dale buzzed from all the alcohol and Beth pretty buzzed herself.

Anyway, it was a *lot* later than Dale had realized and now they were *out of time, damn it,* and that frustration must have tightened like a knot in Dale's chest as they headed back through town, and what with the beer, of course, and his own frustration, Dale must have misjudged his speed or maybe the speed of the Union Pacific passenger train that flew through town at 80 miles per hour every night at 10:05 on its way to the West Coast.

The engineer always blew his whistle all the way through town, but there weren't any lights or guard rails at the crossing in those days like there are now, and Dale's Mustang didn't quite make it. The locomotive caught its rear bumper and spun it back around against the locomotive's wheels and smashed it clean in two, throwing Dale's body more than a hundred feet into a power pole but leaving Beth's in the crushed passenger compartment only a few feet from the tracks. One of the car's wheels went spinning off down the street and broke through the big front window of Mike Davis's father's hardware store, three blocks away.

It took the engineer a mile to get his train stopped.

# # #

Now you may wonder how I happen to know all these things about John and Dale and Beth. After all, I said at the beginning that this is a true story and what I've told you is pretty specific. Well, I know because I'm John. And back then it wasn't "the three of them" but "the three of us."

Anyway, the people who lived near the tracks were so used to the train whistles that echoed through their neighborhoods day and night that they didn't hear them anymore. But they heard the crash sure enough and a lot of them jumped up to see what godawful thing had happened. Harry Johnson's family lived in a little rundown shack a block away, and he and his father and mother pulled on their clothes and hurried out, but later Mrs. Johnson told everyone who would listen that she wished she hadn't seen what she'd seen. There was more of that kind of thing, a lot more, but it all came down to the *same* thing.

Anyway, neighbor called neighbor and word spread, so that by midnight everybody in town and outside of town knew pretty much what had happened and whom it had happened to. My parents, who'd waved out the window that evening at Dale and Beth when they'd picked me up, got one of the later calls and they rushed upstairs to my bedroom to see me lying there peacefully asleep in my bed. They hesitated, but then woke me up and told me the news.

So I got up, brushed my teeth and washed my face and combed my hair and Father drove me down to the police station so I could tell them what I knew. Like that damn cliché has it, it was the first day of the rest of my life.

Offerings

Once I found
the tip of a finger bone
wrapped in gauze
and lying on an attic shelf.
Did I really unwrap it to
see what it was? I
never could bring myself
to touch the cat's carcass
that hung for years
from the pasture fence.

Wrecking Ball

They were tearing down Meirs' Department Store that last week in June. I say Meirs', but long before that, almost before my time, it was C.C. Dennison's Emporium. And later, until it closed last year, it was Lane's, but the name had never quite caught on with me.

A crane with a wrecking ball had been at work since early morning, when I had first walked by, and the operator had plugged away at a slow, steady pace all day. Now the west wall of the building had been reduced to a jumble of twisted steel and shattered concrete, and the operator had started on the south wall, the old brick one. The building occupied about half a block in all. A tobacco shop had once stood across the alley, and I had been a regular customer in my smoking days. I think there had been a candy store too.

O'Hara and I were sitting in the shade across the street on a bench. We often ran into each other this time of day, although neither of us seemed to plan it. We were both alone—he'd been divorced for years and I'd been a widower for even longer. I guess time was heavy on our hands, but we got on well. I would have said that we didn't have to talk to fill the silence, but something about today was different.

The crane took another pass and the ball swung slowly but with great force into the wall. The bricks exploded in a cloud of rubble and dust, exposing a tangle of rebar and sending a sharp crash rolling over us half a second later. The entire structure would surely be a memory by the end of the week. I had read what was going up in its place, but the name escaped me at the moment.

"Old man Dennison used to give kids gum when the place was his," I said to O'Hara. I guess I hated to see the place go, although it had been a long time since it meant anything to me. "He'd see a kid in tow with his mother in Housewares or whatever and flip him a piece of gum. Gave me a piece once. I was shy and didn't know what to do, but my mother thanked him and explained later that Mr. Dennison didn't have any children of his own and so he was always kind to other people's." As I said it, I realized that O'Hara didn't have any children either. I hurried on: "Their restaurant must have been the only place in this part of town where I could meet a client in the middle of the day. At least one who wasn't a boozer."

"The Top o' the Day."

"What?"

"The Top o' the Day. As in, 'The top o' the day to ya.' That's what it was called—in the legal papers anyway. The Top o' the Day Restaurant and Tea Room. I renegotiated the contract when Dennison sold. Of course everybody called it the Topper. After all, it was on the top floor. Call it Top o' the Day and nobody would have known what the hell you were talking about." O'Hara was staring intently at the crane, as if he were going to be tested later on its movements.

"Did you know him well? Meier?" Benjamin J. Meier was Dennison's successor.

"Never saw him outside of business hours," O'Hara said. "I don't think he was cut from the same mold as Dennison. He had one of those big new houses out on the Bench, but I lived downtown. Always did. I was a city boy."

Now a meatloaf sandwich may not be the kind of thing that sticks in your memory, but the talk about the lunch counter had reminded me that whenever I ate there, I ordered a meatloaf sandwich. On rye. I couldn't remember having one since, and what's more hadn't even thought of one. I said as much to O'Hara.

The ball swung and O'Hara turned his head to follow it. "Murphy had the recipe from somebody in Salt Lake City. Oh, sorry, Murphy ran the counter. Claimed the secret was the Worcestershire sauce. A lot of Worcestershire sauce, but no salt. I usually had the corned beef myself."

The whole experience—the pungent cooking smells, the pleasant midday bustle, the light filtering in through a series of high windows on the north wall—washed over me for a few seconds. Then I remembered something else. "That waitress used to kid me. She always knew what I wanted, because I always wanted the same thing."

"Evie."

"Was that her name? I didn't remember."

"Yeah, Evie. Murphy's wife. She ran the staff and waited tables during the rush hour."

There'd been some kind of change along the way, I remembered. The place had fallen out of my routine. "What ever happened to them?"

"Moved to Spokane in '85 to run a restaurant up there. Still do, the last I heard. Near the train depot. But I haven't passed through Spokane for a while."

"Evie! What a perfect name. She was a hot little—" I stopped. That year must have been about the time O'Hara's wife had left him. Or had it been the other way around? We were just getting to know each other then, but I remembered … Actually, I wasn't sure what I remembered, but suddenly I was struck by how little I knew about this man sitting beside me.

The ball swung.

O'Hara didn't say anything for a long time but simply watched the wrecking ball do its work on the brick, back and forth. "Yes ... she was," he finally said, and after a pause turned to me with the question one of us always asked the other toward the end of the afternoon. "You ready for that drink? Gibb's or the Time Out?"

"Gibb's," I said. "That new man at the Time Out mixes a weak drink." Just then the whistle blew and the crane operator began lowering the big ball to the ground. The south wall was gone.

Jones Bros.

The timid
went into shoe repair,
the more aggressive
cut hair a few hours a week
next door. The
slack-jawed, vacant of stare
spent endless afternoons
of drool on the back
porch. The salivary
glands, as the local quack
was fond of observing,
operated at a
perfectly normal rate.

A View of the Owyhees

These things happened a long time ago.

#

Two men, Burt Johnson and George Lawrence, lived with their wives, Florence and Bea, on a country road west of Boise. Burt and George farmed forty acres apiece, which wasn't enough to make a living on, even then, so they had to supplement their income, Burt by plumbing and George by plowing his neighbors' fields.

Burt and George both liked their food, but they were big-boned men who worked long hours, so they carried their weight well. You would often see George driving his tractor down the road toward some field or other, and if you were out front where he could see you, you could count on his lifting his index finger from the wheel in greeting as he rode by. He was a friendly man but he didn't go out of his way to show it.

Burt was more gregarious. If you weren't careful he might stay to talk about one thing or another after he'd fixed your sink and you were anxious to eat lunch. He had a lot of interests besides water and pipes, and might want to mention the latest theory about the origin of Venus that he'd been reading about.

Aside from little differences such as these, Burt and George resembled each other in ways other than size, ways that people found a little hard to define. And the same was true of Florence and Bea. Florence was blonde and Bea brunette, and Florence wore her hair long and Bea not so long, but they had the same demeanor, and people tended to think of them at more or less the same time. They were a type, just like Burt and George were another type.

Burt and George were friends at some largely unspoken level, and so Florence and Bea were friends too. They were often to be found together on Sunday afternoons at one house or the other, and over time one of the topics of conversation between Burt and George was how much each liked the other's house. Burt lived near a big canal, and his back lawn was shaded by willows and cottonwoods. Raccoons were common along the canal, and while he found them a nuisance, George was fascinated by them. Burt, on the other hand, enjoyed visiting George's farm, which was located on a bench of high ground looking out over the Snake River Plain. A man could breathe there, Burt thought when he visited. A man could see the far-off Owyhee Mountains from George's back porch.

It probably wasn't exactly a surprise to those who knew them that one year Burt and George traded farms. They'd talked the arrangement through and discussed the advantages and disadvantages. Being on higher ground, George's farm might have been worth a little more, but his ground was rockier, so the two factors pretty much evened out. So they shook hands, went to see a lawyer, spent a few weeks packing and moving and unpacking, and that was that. I'm sure that the neighbors speculated about the switch, but that was about it. After all, Burt and George were enough alike that it must have seemed as if nothing much had changed.

But there was something more to the situation. Florence and Bea hadn't moved.

It took some time for the fact to sink into people's heads, but whereas Burt had once lived with Florence, now he lived with Bea, and George now lived with Florence. At first, thought the neighbors, the move was just taking more time. But after a month or two it was obvious that there had been not just a swap of farms but of spouses. I'm sure that there were more than a few jokes made and eyebrows raised, but, well, Burt and George were quite a bit alike, and Florence and Bea were quite a bit alike, and I'll bet it seemed as if nothing much had changed. And after another month or two the couples ceased to be of interest. The four of them, the neighbors must have concluded, had found a way of dealing with a situation that, if the truth were known, was not entirely unheard of.

As it turned out, though, things weren't what they seemed, because one Sunday afternoon that first winter, while George was taking a nap, Florence took his double-barreled shotgun from the back of the closet, drove over to what was now Burt and Bea's house and, finding Bea alone on the back porch drinking coffee and staring out at the snow-capped Owyhees, shot her in the back of the head. Then, either immediately or a short time later, she shot herself in the forehead with the other barrel.

#

George and I still get together, but not often. It's been a long time since we talked about what happened, and even then, there wasn't much to be said, except this: Florence had two more shells in her coat pocket that afternoon. Did she plan to shoot me and Bea before returning to her house to take care of George and then herself? I was visiting my brother in Nampa that afternoon—something I seldom did—so we'll never know. At the inquest George swore that Florence had never said a thing, that she'd seemed very happy. I know I had been, and I'm pretty sure my dear Bea had been too, pretty sure. There doesn't seem to be any way of getting at the rest of it.

I retired pretty soon afterward—people felt uncomfortable inviting me into their homes—and George the next spring. I don't think he was ready, but he turned his tractor over one day and that right arm of his has never been the same. As I said, we still get together now and then, but I usually go to his house by the river. When he comes to my house, we always sit out front or, if it's winter, in the living room. We never go out back.

1968

Tires piled out back.
Smell of old oil.
Saturday night and Coors
and fishing Charlie Creek
up north. All that
shit. Male bonding,
I'm told, essential to
the development of the
male psyche. So Frank
shot a buck one morning
and his wife that
night. Her father, the
sheriff, was first
on the scene.

What I Mean?

"Where was I?" Luther asks, looking around at Ray and Tom and me. We were sitting in his back yard under a big catalpa. "Oh, yeah, we'd pulled into this rest stop in Oregon, someplace north of Medford, I dunno, maybe a hundred miles out."

He pauses again. He's having a hard time getting to wherever it is he's going with this, so I say "That's fine country" just to keep things moving along.

"Yeah, well, there was this old couple there, offhand I don't remember their names, but I could look it up, and *that's* part of the point. This all happened."

He takes a gulp of his beer.

"Anyway, an old couple, she looked like she ought to be named Flo, what I mean? Like that. Anyway, they've got this fancy camper with all those decals you get, Sea Lion Caves and all that, and they've set out a couple of aluminum chairs. It is a rest stop, you know, and they're the kind of people you're going to smile at and get right on your way."

He takes another gulp, looks around. "Any of you got a cigarette?"

Ray does, so Luther takes one and lights up, and I do too, although I actually quit a few years back. Luther takes a deep drag and almost launches into a coughing fit but manages to catch himself.

"Plus, they got this dog, this Pomeranian." He spits the word out. "They call 'em *Poms*. Christ I hate those dogs! Little goddamn things the size of a, I dunno, *a rat*. Mean little things too, they got these teeth like … Anyway, I see this Pomeranian and I'm definitely on my way, but Sara, she *likes* 'em, so she walks right up and starts petting the thing and of course it starts quivering all over, like it's *palsied*. Christ!"

He finishes his beer, reaches another one out of the cooler and pops the tab, takes a long pull.

"Well, Sara starts talking to them and it turns out they're from Eagle. I mean that's a hell of a coincidence, here we are in the middle of Oregon, and they're from Eagle. Eagle, Idaho. I mean, I grew up there, moved away years ago, but I'm thinking, hell, they're old enough, they might have known my parents. That used to happen every so often there for a while, I'd run into somebody who knew my parents."

"Well, I started listening up then. But there wasn't anything to hear, it turned out they'd moved to Eagle long after our time—but when it was still small, they said. *Small!* I remember when it was so small, hell, people moved out, not in. Anyway, I got us outta there, kept going till we got where we were going. End of story, what I mean? Nothing to remember."

Luther has this habit of saying "What I mean?" instead of "You know what I mean?" when he gets carried away, and it makes it a little hard to follow his train of thought.

"Except there was. That damn dog, that's what. That's why I knew it was the same people when I read that story in the paper last week. The old couple that disappeared? Hell, I wouldn't have given it a thought except that the story mentioned their dog. *A Pomeranian.* This old couple were due home in Eagle, never showed up, their kids were worried, yadda yadda. *And they had a Pomeranian.* They're the ones we saw in Medford!"

"Huh!" says Ray, who I hadn't thought was paying attention. He's on his fourth or fifth beer, and that's a problem that's gonna have to be taken care of sometime, we're all hoping by Ray himself, but we'll see. Anyway, we're all properly impressed by this coincidence of Luther's, but he's not done.

"So they found 'em last week, you know," Luther says.

"I didn't see that," I say, and apparently Ray and Tom haven't either, but they're paying a little more attention now, at least Tom is, because it sounds like the story might actually be going someplace.

"Yeah, way out by some dry creek about a dozen miles off the road. No clue why. Anyway, the old man had apparently flipped the truck over into the streambed, musta killed the old woman instantly, but he crawled out a way, had a broken leg, but he didn't get far."

"Huh." Ray again, looking a little dazed.

"Yeah, both of 'em dead. Nobody knows what they coulda been doing. Looking for petrified wood? But here's the clincher. The damn dog *lived*. The Pom."

"Huh!" Tom this time.

"Yeah, the Pom. And you know what its name was?"

We didn't know what its name was.

"Toto. *Toto*, for God's sake. Like in that movie, uh, *The Wizard of Oz*."

"That was some kinda terrier, I think." I don't know why I mentioned it, it's not like it mattered.

"Whatever," says Luther. "The thing is, I've always *hated* that movie, hated what's-her-name, Judy Garland, hated the dog. And here's this poor old couple, moved to my hometown, dead, nobody knows why, but this damn *Toto* gets to live. There was this picture in the paper."

I didn't point out how he felt about the poor old couple when he met them. The story seemed to be about something else.

"Makes me wanna puke," Luther goes on. "I mean, what's the point? The kids'll take the dog in, maybe the grandkids, here's this heart-rending reminder of what happened to the old folks. Show up in *Reader's Digest* for all I know."

"They still publish that?" Ray asks.

Luther shakes his head. "Hell, I don't know. But the thing is—" He rubs his hands up and down his face. "I just don't know what to—" He's staring into the cooler now and his mouth's hanging open. "Christ, Ray, you've drunk all the beer!" Then he rubs his face again, like he wants to rub something away.

Where

No, the boom
never reached this far.
The freeway passed twelve
miles south of here.
The spur rusted.
Maybe you got away,
whoever you are.
I never did.

The Other Side

I took one of my favorite hikes late last season, up to Cramer Lakes in the Sawtooths. The lakes lie at an altitude of almost 8,400 feet, and Redfish Lake—that's where you start up—is a little over 6,500 feet, so it's what's called an "accessible" hike. There are much harder ones in the area, believe me, but it's a full day up and a day back, and I spend another day poking around and shooting some photos and maybe hooking a few fish, so it's a good three days in all.

I'd parked behind the lodge, eaten a big breakfast and talked for a few minutes on the dock with one of the other hikers, an older fellow, before setting out on the shuttle. He had a weathered look about him, along with decades-old clothes and jacket to match, and we made the kind of small talk you make when you're going to be in a stranger's company for a while. I mentioned where I was going, and he replied that he was headed to Madeline Lake. I nodded, hating to reveal my ignorance, since I've lived in the Stanley Basin for decades, but the truth is I'd never heard of Madeline Lake. (On top of everything else, I'm guessing that's how it's spelled, since there's more than one way.)

It was a crisp morning—they're always crisp here when they aren't downright freezing—but I've never found the five-mile boat ride across the lake to the trailhead unpleasant. It's a restful prelude to the hike, and a good chance for me to clear my mind of the extraneous thoughts that are normally crowding it.

I'm going to call the old man "Joe," since I need a handle for him, and somehow, he looked like a Joe. In any case, our routes apparently lay together up the cleared trail through the valley floor for the first part of the climb, so I let him take the lead. Whatever concerns I might have had about his age, he didn't seem to have any trouble with the climb, but after about half an hour, he sat down on a boulder to retie his boots. As I joined him on a nearby boulder, he fumbled open the pocket of his flannel shirt to take something out. I assumed it would be a map, but when I glanced over, he was holding what looked like a snapshot.

"My wife," Joe explained. "She asked me to keep her picture with me."

I nodded, but all I had seen was a pale rectangle.

"She says things are a little ... indistinct there," he continued.

He stared at the snapshot, and I had the impression that he would have kissed it if I hadn't been there. I turned away.

"Well, this is where I turn off," Joe finally said, putting the photo away and nodding toward a wooded ridge that rose alongside the trail ahead of us. "I'm headed for the other side."

I wished him luck and he raised his hand in farewell as he began working his way through the brush around a deadfall at the tip of the ridge. Could there be an unmarked trail there? I thought about checking, but I didn't want to lose my momentum, so I continued on my way.

# # #

Finishing a long hike is as satisfying as starting it, and I try to stretch out the pleasure for as long as possible. In this case, I visited the bar that runs along the side of the lodge, an unpretentious little place that can't have changed much since the lodge was built in 1929. I was looking forward to a quiet hour nursing a beer, resting my boots on the fender of the fireplace and thinking over the hike as the evening set in.

I'd set up my tent in a good spot between the upper and lower lakes and enjoyed a big meal of pan-fried trout the second night. And I'd gotten some good panoramic shots of the Stanley Basin that I would work up back home. But thinking about my photographs reminded me of Joe and his snapshot, if that's really what it had been. It wasn't important, but the incident puzzled me. Like I said, all I'd seen was a pale, empty rectangle. When I'd questioned the shuttle pilot on the way back an hour before, he didn't think that he'd seen Joe since that first morning, so maybe the man knew another way out. Or maybe he was still up there. His pack, which had looked about as old as he was, wasn't that big, so he'd have to be eating a lot of trout.

#

A few days later I had some business at the ranger station and thought I'd ask the ranger about Madeline Lake. He hadn't heard of it either, but that wasn't conclusive.

"I learn something every day," he explained. I knew from long experience that he tended to talk in clichés.

"Let's see," he continued, taking one book and then another off the shelves behind his desk. I recognized all of them, but didn't say anything. Next, he pulled open a wide drawer and lifted out some topos—topographical maps. I'd tried those too, but it was reassuring to see someone else going through the same motions.

Finally the ranger turned to his computer and checked a USGS database of place names. I recognized its layout immediately.

"Huh!" He shook his head and finally turned back to me. "Maybe the fellow knows something we don't."

Thinking that I couldn't have put it better myself, I thanked the ranger and headed back to my pickup. The first storm of the season was on the way, and I wanted to get home before it hit.

Notes on Place Names

Boise is the capital of Idaho. "All Boise names are transferred from the name given the river by French-Canadian explorers and trappers for the great variety of trees growing along its banks. After traveling over many miles of arid land, they are said to have exclaimed, 'Les bois, les bois! Voyes les bois!' (The woods, the woods! See the woods!)." Lalia Boone, *Idaho Place Names: A Geographical Dictionary*, 1988

The Boise Bench consists of "the first and second plateaus south of Boise's historic city center." Angie K. Davis, *The Boise Bench History Project, 2020.*

The Boise Front is a series of foothills in Ada County, Idaho, stretching from Eagle in the north to a reservoir on the Boise River known as Lucky Peak in the south.

Coeur d'Alene is located on the northern shore of Lake Coeur d'Alene in northern Idaho. Its name "was first given the Indians of the area by French fur trappers and traders. It has been interpreted in a variety of ways: 'awl,' 'pointed,' or 'needle-hearted,' for the shrewd trading ability of the Indians." Boone, *op cit.*

Cramer Lakes, Idaho: "In less than 8 miles (14+ roundtrip), the trail to Cramer Lakes transports you away from the accessible Redfish Lake Lodge to a secluded and beautiful chain of alpine lakes." Amanda Solomon, *The Outbound.*

Eagle, Idaho, is "a town located 5.3 mi E of Star, ½ mi N of the Boise River.... Named for the bald eagle, which used this area as habitat." Boone, *op cit.*

"Idaho is a coined word. It has no origin in any known Indian language, despite the popular belief that it was originally Ee-da-how—'Light on the Mountain.'" Boone, op cit. Before the arrival of European-American usurpers, it was home to a number of Native American Peoples "divided into five distinct groups:

the Kutenai (sometimes called Kootenai), Coeur d'Alene, and Nez Perce in the North, the Shoshoni and Northern Paiute in the south." *Idaho State Historical Reference Series*, no. 22.

Madeline Lake has never been identified.

Medford is the county seat of Jackson County in southwestern Oregon.

Nampa, Idaho, is "the largest city in Canyon County." Boone, *op cit.*

Oregon lies west of Idaho.

The Owyhee Mountain Range "extends from Oregon into Owyhee County [Idaho] in a SW direction for about 60 mi, varying in width from 10 to 35 mi." The range is named for "three Owyhees" (natives of the Hawaiian Islands) who left a trapping party in the early 19th century "to explore … unknown terrain. They never returned." Boone, *op cit.*

Redfish Lake, Idaho, is the "largest body of water in Sawtooth area; S of Stanley between Salmon River and Sawtooth Mountains.… Named for the sockeye salmon found here." Boone, *op ci*t.

The Sawtooth Mountains "include the ranges and masses around the heads of Salmon River, the S Fk Boise River, and Big Wood River. The most magnificent group of mountains in Idaho.… Named for the rugged peaks that from a distance look like the serrated teeth of a saw." Boone, *op cit.*

Sea Lion Caves is a system of sea caves on the Pacific Ocean coast of Oregon that attracts numerous sea lions. The caves "were discovered in 1880 by a local seaman, Captain William, Cox, who entered the grotto through the western channel in a small boat on a calm day." *Wikipedia.* The caves have since become a popular tourist attraction.

The Snake River is "one of the largest rivers in the United States" and is "named for the Snake tribe of Shoshoni Indians." Boone, *op cit.*

Spokane "is the most populous city in eastern Washington." *Wikipedia*

The Stanley Basin is a "[d]epression in SW part of Custer County [Idaho] extending S and W from the confluence of the upper portion of the Salmon River and Valley Creek.... Named for John Stanley, the oldest man in an 1863 prospecting party, who struck pay dirt in this area." Boone, *op cit.*

Grove Koger grew up in rural Idaho and earned a BA from the College of Idaho and an MLibr from the University of Washington's School of Librarianship. Before his retirement, he worked as a librarian in public and academic libraries, and in 1999 won the Allie Beth Martin Award, presented by the Public Library Association and Baker & Taylor to "a librarian who, in a pubic library setting, has demonstrated ... extraordinary range and depth of knowledge about books or other library materials; and ... distinguished ability to share that knowledge." Besides writing for a number of reference works, Koger has published articles, short stories, and poems in journals in the United States and abroad. He is the author of a readers' guide to travel narratives, *When the Going Was Good*; a chapbook of poetry, *Not*; and two chapbooks of short stories, *Something Strange* and *Treacherous Waters*. His play *Ruby Testifies* was performed at the Black Box Theatre in Bloomington, Indiana, in 1990. He was Assistant Editor of Art Patron Magazine and Contributing Editor for Books with *Boise Magazine*, and is currently Assistant Editor of *Deus Loci: The Lawrence Durrell Journal*. He lives in Boise, Idaho, with his wife, poet Margaret Koger.

www.ingramcontent.com/pod-product-compliance
Lightning Source LLC
Chambersburg PA
CBHW022044080426
42734CB00009B/1235